Uktub
al-'arabiya

Uktub al-'arabiya

BEGINNERS WRITING SKILLS
IN MODERN STANDARD ARABIC

Azza Hassanein
Dalal Abo El Seoud
Hala Yehia

The American University in Cairo Press
Cairo • New York

Dar el Kutub No. 13676/12
ISBN 978 977 416 585 6

Dar el Kutub Cataloging-in-Publication Data

Hassanein, Azza
    Uktub al-'arabiya: Beginners Writing Skills in Modern Standard Arabic/ Azza Hassanein, Dalal Abo El Seoud, Hala Yehia.—Cairo: The American University in Cairo Press, 2013.
    p.   cm.
    ISBN 978 977 416 585 6
    1. Arabic Language study and teaching.
    I. Abo El Seoud, Dalal (jt. auth.)
    II. Yehia, Hala (jt. auth.)
    492.7

1 2 3 4 5   17 16 15 14 13

Designed by Cherif Abdullah
Printed in Egypt

المحتويات

Introduction 1

كلمة للمدرسين ٣

Plan of the Book 5

الوحدة الأولى: أنا

الدرس الأول: الأبراج الأرقام العربية، الشهور، التاريخ، الأبراج ١٣

الدرس الثاني: رحلات مصر للطيران أيام الأسبوع، البلاد، العواصم، الجنسية، مفردات عن البلاد، الضمائر المتصلة ١٩

الدرس الثالث: في غرفة الصف العلاقات المكانية: مفردات عن غرفة الصف ظرف المكان، جمل اسمية بسيطة ٢٧

الدرس الرابع: الصفات (١) الوصف: الصفات، الجملة الاسمية بالخبر المفرد، المذكر والمؤنث ٣٣

الدرس الخامس: تسالي (مراجعة) مراجعة: الأسعار والنقود، مفردات عن الأماكن اليومية ٣٨

الوحدة الثانية: أنا والأسرة والأصدقاء

الدرس السادس: تعارف (١) التعريف بالذات وبالآخر، أفعال ٤٩

الدرس السابع: تعارف (٢) إيجاد معلومات، تكوين الأسئلة
والرد عليها ٥٥

الدرس الثامن: الأسرة الكتابة عن الأسرة، أفعال، عند + ضمير أدوات
الربط: و، أيضًا، ثم، بالإضافة إلى ذلك ٦٠

الدرس التاسع: الأصدقاء استخدام المعلومات لكتابة فقرة أدوات الربط:
لكن، ولكن، إنما، لكنه، لكنها ٦٦

الدرس العاشر: الصفات (٢) كتابة فقرة لوصف الأصدقاء، مفردات جسم
الإنسان الجملة الاسمية، الخبر المقدم، أدوات الربط: أما . . . فـ . . . ٧٣

الدرس الحادي عشر: أنا والأسرة والأصدقاء العلاقات الزمنية: ظرف
الزمان (مراجعة) ٧٩

الوحدة الثالثة: أنا وبيتي وشارعي

الدرس الثاني عشر: بيتي (١) وصف المكان: وصف البيت،
الخبر المقدم ٨٥

الدرس الثالث عشر: بيتي (٢) وصف المكان: أدوات ربط للمقارنة،
اسم التفضيل ٩٢

الدرس الرابع عشر: في الشارع وصف الشارع: مفردات المحال في
الشارع، أدوات ربط لتوضيح العلاقات المكانية ٩٧

الوحدة الرابعة: ماذا أفعل وماذا فعلت وماذا كنت أفعل؟

الدرس الخامس عشر: يوم الإجازة السرد للأحداث اليومية: كتابة النشاط اليومي، المضارع،أحب أن، من اللازم أن، من الممكن أن   ١٠٧

الدرس السادس عشر: أمس في المطعم السرد في الماضي: الفعل الماضي، أدوات ربط للسرد الزمني، متلازمات، وصف المكان   ١١٥

الدرس السابع عشر: اسمها ليلى السرد في الماضي المستمر: كان، أدوات ربط للتتابع، متلازمات، حروف جر مع أفعال   ١٢٢

INTRODUCTION

The main objective of *Uktub al-'arabiya: Beginners Writing Skills in Modern Standard Arabic*, the first in a series of three books, including intermediate and advanced levels, is to raise learners' *awareness* of Arabic-language structures to allow them to form correct words, phrases, sentences, and to write simple texts. This is achieved in several ways:

- Stating specific objectives at the outset of each of the book's seventeen lessons.
- Introducing useful words, as well as illustrations and drills, to help students with the lesson. This will help students to use words in context rather than memorizing them in separate lists.
- Using inductive drills, whereby students explore sentences to guess rules of grammar. By doing so, their awareness of correct linguistic structures is raised.
- Asking students to reflect at the end of each lesson on what they have learned, what they still need to ask the teacher about, and finally what extra information they need to know, thus developing their metacognition
- After they have completed their homework, students are asked to assess themselves by specifically checking the main points related to the lesson's objectives.
- From Lesson 12 onward, guessing strategies instead of vocabulary lists are used to enable students to improve their vocabulary.

By the end of this book, students will be able to:

1- Combine letters to form words.
2- Construct phrases, such as: الإضافة – الصفة والموصوف – الجار والمجرور
3- Use simple collocations and expressions in the final few lessons
4- Recombine familiar words to form new structures.
5- Write simple sentences (such as questions and descriptions).
6- Use simple connectors to punctuate sentences.
7- Combine sentences to form simple cohesive paragraphs.
8- Assess their own and their peers' writing.

كلمة للمدرسين

- يبدأ كل درس بتوضيح الأهداف المرجو تحقيقها منه، وقد كتبت بالإنجليزية حتى يتعرف عليها الطالب أيضًا.

- تبدأ الدروس بالتركيز على الأعداد وبعض المفردات الهامة وذلك في المرحلة التمهيدية التي يتعلم الطالب فيها الألف باء.

- يبدأ كل درس وحتى الدرس الثاني عشر بمفردات مهمة، يقوم الطالب بتوظيفها في التدريبات، وذلك بغرض تعلمها من خلال السياق وليس من خلال قوائم منفردة.

- تم الاعتماد في بداية الكتاب على دروس تحتوي على نصوص لإعلانات أصلية، ثم تلاها فقرات شبه أصلية تخدم الموضوعات والتراكيب المطروحة. وانتهى الكتاب بنص أصلي بغرض إعداد الطلاب للمستوى التالي.

- تقوم التدريبات على توظيف استراتيجية التخمين أولًا ثم إعمال الذهن والتطبيق بعد ذلك، بدءًا من الكلمة فالعبارة ثم انتقالًا للجملة والفقرة القصيرة.

- تقوم التدريبات أيضًا على استراتيجيات القراءة مثل التصفح لإيجاد المعلومات، واستخدام الخلفيات والسياق والمعلومات اللغوية لتخمين معاني المفردات.

- تم توظيف الصور بشكل واسع في الكتاب لتعطي المعنى وتشجع على استراتيجيات التخمين والفهم، كما تساعد على تيسير الفهم.

- تم الاهتمام بأدوات الربط من الدروس الأولى وذلك لتدريب الطلاب وتعويدهم على تكوين فقرة مترابطة الجمل من البداية.

- في نهاية كل درس يقوم الطالب بتقديم انطباعاته عن الدرس بالنسبة لما تعلمه وتمكن منه إلى جانب ما يواجهه من مشكلات، وأخيرًا المعلومات الإضافية التي يريد أن يُلم بها. يلي ذلك وبعد الانتهاء من عمل الواجب كتابة تقييم ذاتي للتأكد من فهمه لكل النقاط التي تناولها الدرس.

Structures	Activities
Idaafa phrases	– Identifying months – Writing months corresponding to horoscopes – Seeking information from peers – Writing birth dates and birth signs
Nationality adjectives	– Finding country names – Finding days of the week – Forming nationality adjectives – Seeking information from peers – Writing questions
– Adverbs of place – Nominal sentences	– Identifying vocabulary – Searching for vocabulary – Filling in blanks with classroom items and adverbs
Simple nominal sentences	– Choosing the correct adjectives – Writing opposites – Writing simple sentences

PLAN OF THE BOOK

		Goals	Functions
Unit 1	**I**		
Lesson 1	Horoscope Signs	Writing numbers, months of the year, dates, and horoscope signs	Increasing vocabulary for the description of time such as months of the year and birthdays.
Lesson 2	Egypt Air Trips	Recognizing and writing names of countries, nationality adjectives, days of the week	Increasing vocabulary for narration of time
Lesson 3	In the Classroom	Knowing and writing classroom vocabulary and adverbs of place	– Describing a classroom – Using adverbs of place
Lesson 4	Descriptions (1)	Knowing and writing some adjectives	Describing people
Lesson 5	Entertainment (Revision)		

Structures	Activities
Nominal sentence	– Sentence completion – Sentence formation – Information gathering – Question writing – Constructing business cards – Preparing questions
Questions for narration	– Choosing question words – Completing sentences with question words – Rearranging questions – Forming questions – Translating questions – Providing questions for answers to create an interview – Transforming an interview into narrative
– Nominal sentences – Adjectives and adverbs – Conjugation of عند	– Fill in the spaces – Match questions and answers – Provide questions – Build sentences – Visualization – Using an illustration to describe a family member
– Noun-adjective structures – More about nominal sentences	– Adjective identification – Writing short sentences using adjectives
– Nominal sentences – Using connectors	– Using information to draw a picture – Converting the picture into short descriptive paragraph – Using illustrations to complete sentences – Describing own family

		Goals	Functions
Unit 2	**Family, Friends, and I**		
Lesson 6	Getting Acquainted (1)	Writing information about oneself and others	Writing about oneself
Lesson 7	Getting Acquainted (2)	Writing questions for making an acquaintance	Writing about others
Lesson 8	Family	Describing people	–Writing about family members – Using adverbs of time
Lesson 9	Friends	Describing people and objects	Using adjectives to write descriptions
Lesson 10	Description (2)	Knowing more adjectives and names body parts	Using adjectives to describe people using more complex sentences
Lesson 11	Family, Friends, and I (Revision)		

Structures	Activities
Using adjectives and adverbs for writing descriptions	– Guessing meaning – Classification of vocabulary – Writing dialogues – Finding collocations – Describing an apartment – Using connectors – Comparing – Free writing
Using connectors to show differences and similarities	– Describing places – Forming questions and seeking information – Describing the apartment – Guessing the meanings of connectors – Comparing apartments – Using adverbs to describe streets
Using adverbs of place and names of shops to describe streets	– Identifying vocabulary – Guessing – Using connectors to connect sentences – Visualizing – Describing streets
– Present tense – Using أنْ with verbs – Using لـ with verbs	– Guessing verb meanings – Using the present tense in sentences – Completing sentences – Creating dialogues – Writing about vacations
– Past tense verbs – Using connectors	– Sentence building – Converting sentences into a story – Writing collocations – Answering questions – Converting dialogue into paragraphs – Using the five senses to describe a place
– Continuous past tense structures – Using adverbs of time – Using connectors	– Brainstorming for past tense verbs – Writing sentences using the past tense – Narrating a story in the past tense

		Goals	Functions
Unit 3	**My Home, My Street, and I**		
Lesson 12	My Home (1)	Describing different rooms in the house and items in each room	Describing your house
Lesson 13	My Home (2)	More description of rooms in the house; comparing different houses	Describing your house and the street you live in
Lesson 14	In the Street	Describing streets and shops	Describing the street
Unit 4	**What I Do, What I Did, What I Used to Do**		
Lesson 15	A Day Off	Describing activities in the vacation	Narrating using the present tense
Lesson 16	Yesterday in the Restaurant	Describing past activities	Narrating using the past tense
Lesson 17	Her name is Layla	Describing past con-tinuous activities	Narrating using continuous past tense

الوحدة الأولى

أنا

الـدرس الأول

الأبراج

Horoscope Signs

Objectives:

After completing this lesson, students will be able to write:

1- Numbers.
2- Months of the year.
3- Dates.
4- Horoscope signs.

Useful words and numbers:

10	9	8	7	6	5	4	3	2	1	0
١٠	٩	٨	٧	٦	٥	٤	٣	٢	١	٠
عشرة	تسعة	ثمانية	سبعة	ستة	خمسة	أربعة	ثلاثة	اثنان	واحد	صفر

1- Look at the table above and supply the Arabic numbers as in the example:

7800	156	94	32	11
				١١

2- Ask three of your colleagues for their mobile numbers and write them in the chart as in the example below:

رقم التليفون	الإسم
٠١٠٠٥٨٥٦١٥٥	جون John

3- Look at the chart below and write down the horoscope signs associated with the months listed on page 16:

السرطان 21 June – 22 July	الجوزاء 21 May – 20 June	الثور 20 April – 20 May	الحمل 21 March – 19 April
٢١ يونيو – ٢٢ يوليو	٢١ مايو – ٢٠ يونيو	٢٠ ابريل – ٢٠ مايو	٢١ مارس – ١٩ ابريل
العقرب 23 October – 21 November	الميزان 23 September – 22 October	العذراء 23 August – 22 September	الأسد 23 July – 22 August
٢٣ أكتوبر – ٢١ نوفمبر	٢٣ سبتمبر – ٢٢ أكتوبر	٢٣ أغسطس– ٢٢ سبتمبر	٢٣ يوليو – ٢٢ أغسطس
الحوت 19 February – 22 March	الدلو 20 January – 18 February	الجدي 22 December – 21 January	القوس 22 November – 21 December
١٩ فبراير – ٢٢ مارس	٢٠ يناير – ١٨ فبراير	٢٢ ديسمبر – ١٩ يناير	٢٢ نوفمبر – ٢١ ديسمبر

مارس _____ / _____   مايو _____ / _____
يناير _____ / _____   سبتمبر _____ / _____
ديسمبر _____ / _____   فبراير _____ / _____
أبريل _____ / _____   يونيو _____ / _____
أغسطس _____ / _____   أكتوبر _____ / _____
يوليو _____ / _____   نوفمبر _____ / _____

4- Now write the months covered by the following horoscope signs:

٢– الأسد : _____   ١– الحوت: _____
٤– السرطان: _____   ٣– الثور : _____
٦– العقرب: _____   ٥– الجدي: _____

5- In pairs: (a) connect the letters to work out the months; and (b) find out if any of your peers' birthdays fall in these months:

_____   (ي / و / ن / ي / و) :
_____   (م / ١ / ي / و) :
_____   (أ / غ / س / ط / س) :
_____   (د / ي / س / م / ب / ر) :

Useful Words

the horoscope sign/signs البرج (ج) الأبراج
the name الاسم • your birthday عيد ميلادك
the month الشهر • the day اليوم • date of birth تاريخ الميلاد
the year السنة

6- Now write down names of five of your peers and their dates of birth as in the example below:

اليوم / الشهر / السنة	تاريخ الميلاد	الاسم
١٩٩٥/١١/١٥	١٥ نوفمبر ١٩٩٥	كريم

7- Write down your sign برجكِ / برجكَ **and that of a special person, then write down the date of your birthday** (عيد ميلادك) **and that of his/her birthday under each sign:**

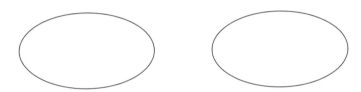

Reflection:

Having completed this lesson, I know:

_____

_____

I still have trouble with the following:

_____

_____

I still need to know more about the following:

_____

_____

Homework الواجب :

You tend to forget the birthdays of your family members and your close friends. Use the following table to keep a record, as in the example:

البرج	اليوم / الشهر / السنة	تاريخ الميلاد	الاسم
العذراء	١٩٩٥/٩/١٥	١٥ سبتمبر ١٩٩٥	منى

Self assessment:

Having completed this lesson, check what you can do:

1- Write Arabic numbers correctly.   (   )

2- Write months of the year easily.   (   )

3- Write dates in correct word order   (   )

4- Write some horoscope signs.   (   )

5- I understand and can write all new words introduced in the lesson.   (   )

الدرس الثاني

رحلات مصر للطيران

Egypt Air Trips

Objectives:
After completing this lesson, students will be able to write

1- Days of the week.
2- Names of some countries and their capitals.
3- Nationality adjectives.
4- Names of some travel destinations.

Useful Words

رحلة (ج) رحلات trip/trips • مصر للطيران Egypt Air
أسبوعياً weekly • مدينة:city • يوم (ج) أيام day/days • يومياً Daily
أيام الأسبوع days of the week • السبت Saturday • الأحد Sunday
الاثنين Monday • الثلاثاء Tuesday • الأربعاء Wednesday
الخميس Thursday • الجمعة Friday • عدا except • البلد the country
المعنى the meaning • الجامعة the university • المكتبة the library

---

مصر للطيران

دبى	الاثنين والثلاثاء والخميس والجمعة والأحد
رأس الخيمة	الخميس
الظهران	يومياً
الرياض	الأربعاء، والجمعة
جدة	يومياً
صنعاء	الاثنين والجمعة
عمـان	يومياً
مسقط	الاثنين والثلاثاء والأربعاء
بيروت	الثلاثاء / الجمعة / السبت
دمشق	الاثنين والأربعاء والخميس والسبت
حلب	الأحـــــد

٨٩ رحلة أسبوعياً إلى ٢٠ مدينة في آسيا والشرقين الأقصى والأوسط

طوكيو	الثلاثاء، الجمعة
مانيلا	الثلاثاء، الجمعة
بانكوك	الثلاثاء، الجمعة
بومباى	السبت
كراتشى	الاثنين الجمعة
الكويت	يومياً
البحرين	الأربعاء، الأحد
الدوحة	يومياً
أبو ظبى	يومياً عدا الثلاثاء
الشارقة	الأربعاء، والخميس

1- Look at the chart above and list all flight destinations on the given days, then guess the meanings of the names of the countries you wrote down:

	السبت	الأحد	الاثنين	الثلاثاء	الأربعاء	الخميس	الجمعة
البلد							
المعنى							
البلد							
المعنى							
البلد							
المعنى							
البلد							
المعنى							
البلد							
المعنى							
البلد							
المعنى							
البلد							
المعنى							

							البلد
							المعنى
							البلد
							المعنى
							البلد
							المعنى
							البلد
							المعنى
							البلد
							المعنى
							البلد
							المعنى
							البلد
							المعنى

2- a) Which day of the week has the highest number of trips?_____

   b) Write the number of trips: _____

3- a) Which day of the week has the lowest number of trips? _____

   b) Write the number of trips: _____

4- Now look and find out on which days of the week there are flights to the following countries (look for their capitals):

اليابان : _____   الإمارات: _____

الهند : _____   الأردن: _____

لبنان : _____   ماليزيا : _____

اليمن: _____   سوريا: _____

البحرين: _____   السعودية : _____

5- Complete the given chart filling in names of countries, cities, and nationalities (masculine and feminine)

Nationality الجنسية	City المدينة	Country البلد
كويتيّ / كويتية		
/	عمَّان	
/		اليابان
سوري / سوريَّة	حلب	
/		اليمن
/		الهند
/		
لبنانيّ /	بيروت	
/		الإمارات

6- Can you work out the rule for deriving the nationality from the name of the country ?

Write it down: _____

7- Find out information about your peers and complete the following table:

His / her nationality جنسيته / جنسيتها	His / her state / town ولايته / ولايتها – بلدته / بلدتها	His / her country بلده / بلدها	His/ her name اسمه / اسمها

Reflection:

Having completed this lesson, I know:

_____

_____

I still have trouble with the following:

_____

_____

I still need to know more about the following:

_____

_____

Homework الواجب :

1- From the following pictures, complete the chart on page 25 by:

  a) writing down the days of the week

  b) writing where you went on each day

الأيام Days	الأماكن Places
ســ	
جـ	
ثا	
خـ	
حـ	
ذ	
ر	

2- Look at the Internet and complete the given table:

Tourist destination مكان سياحيّ	Currency العُملة	Language اللغة	Continent القارة	Capital العاصمة	Country البلد

Self assessment:

Having completed this lesson check what you can do:

1- I know how to write down the days of the week. ( )

2- I know the names of the countries introduced in this lesson. ( )

3- I can derive nationality adjectives from names of countries. ( )

4- I am aware of the difference between masculine and feminine
   nationality adjectives. ( )

5- I know how to write the names of some places that I visit. ( )

6- I understand and can write all the new words introduced in the lesson. ( )

الدرس الثالث

في غرفة الصف

In the Classroom

Objectives:

After completing this lesson the students will be able to write

1- Some classroom vocabulary.
2- Adverbs of place.
3- Simple nominal sentences.

Useful Words

chair كرسي • desk/office مكتب • the classroom غرفة الصف
lamp لمبة • blackboard سبورة • door باب • window نافذة
floor أرض • wall حائط • air condition مكيّف • computer كمبيوتر
teacher مدرسة • trash bin سلة مهملات • bulletin board لوحة إعلانات • student طالب
clock ساعة • students الطلاب • student طالبة • student طالب
closet خزانة • flag علم • flower pot إناء زهور • books كتب • book كتاب
the الـ • picture صورة

1- Look at the illustration below and write down ten items shown in it:

في الصورة ــــــــــــ ، ــــــــــــ ، ــــــــــــ ، ــــــــــــ ، ــــــــــــ

ــــــــــــ ، ــــــــــــ ، ــــــــــــ ، ــــــــــــ ، ــــــــــــ

ــــــــــــ ، ــــــــــــ ، ــــــــــــ ، ــــــــــــ ، ــــــــــــ

ــــــــــــ ، ــــــــــــ ، ــــــــــــ ، ــــــــــــ ، ــــــــــــ

2- Obtain the Arabic equivalents of the English words listed below by readng this chart across and diagonally:

ك	ر	س	ي	ش	ص	ن	و
م	ت	ق	ن	ة	ع	ا	س
ب	م	ب	ا	ب	ل	ج	ب
ي	أ	ي	غ	ث	م	ق	و
و	ر	ط	ا	ل	ب	ظ	ر
ت	ض	ر	م	د	ر	س	ة
ر	خ	ز	ا	ن	ة	ذ	ح
ك	هـ	ف	ن	ا	ف	ذ	ة
إ	ن	ا	ء	ز	هـ	و	ر
س	ل	ة	م	هـ	م	لا	ت

Chair	Computer	Closet
Door	Teacher	Floor
Books	Trash bin	Flower pot
Window	Clock	Flag
Student		

3- Go around your classroom to see if you can find any of the above items, then write them down:

_____

_____

_____

_____

4- Look at the illustration on page 28 and use the words you wrote down as well as the useful adverbs in the box below to fill in the blanks, as shown in the example:

Useful adverbs:	
some	بعض
in front of	أمام
behind	خلف
on	على
above	فوق
below	تحت
beside	بجانب
in/at	في
inside	داخل
outside	خارج
between	بين
to the right of	إلى يمين
to the left of	إلى يسار

١. المدرسة أمام الطلاب.

٢. الكمبيوتر على _____ .

٣. بعض _____ خارج غرفة الصف.

٤. الخزانة إلى يسار _____ .

٥. سلة المهملات _____ المكتب.

٦. _____ فوق _____ .

٧. _____ _____ المدرسة.

٨. لوحة الإعلانات _____ _____ .

٩. _____ إلى يمين المدرسة.

١٠. _____ _____ الحائط.

Reflection:

Having completed this lesson, I know:

_____

_____

I still have trouble with the following:

_____

_____

I still need to know more about the following:

_____

_____

Homework الواجب:

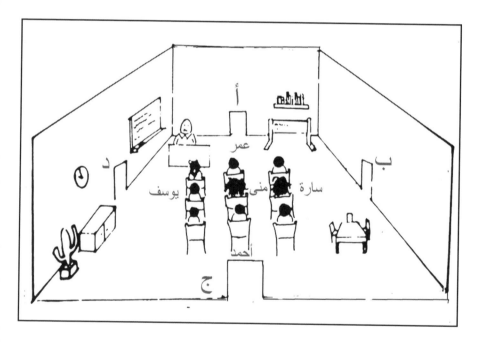

a) Mona has a bad memory. She usually forgets where she sits and what is in her class. Can you help her to remember by completing the following sentences with the correct adverbs:

١– منى _____ سارة ويوسف.

٢– منى _____ عمر.

٣– منى _____ سارة.

٤– منى _____ يوسف.

b) Let's also remind Mona where things are in the class:

٥– السبورة _____ الحائط.

٦– الساعة _____ الخزانة.

٧– إناء الزهور _____.

٨– باب (أ) _____ الطلاب.

٩– باب (ج) _____.

١٠– باب (ب) _____ الطلاب.

c) Draw a classroom with eight items in it, then indicate where each item is in relation to the other items.

1- _____

2- _____

3- _____

4- _____

5- _____

6- _____

7- _____

8- _____

Self assessment:

Having completed this lesson check what you can do:

1- I know how to identify and write down at least ten names of items
   in the classroom.   (   )

2- I know and can write down adverbs of place.   (   )

3- I can write simple sentences using adverbs of place.   (   )

الدرس الرابع

الصفات (١)

Description (1)

Objectives:
After completing this lesson, the students will be able to write some adjectives and simple nominal sentences.

Useful Words

big/old كبير • short قصير • tall/long طويل
fat بدين/سمين • slow بطيء • fast سريع • small/young صغير
old, ancient (non-human) قديم • but she ولكنَّها • thin نحيف
ugly قبيح • handsome وسيم • beautiful جميل • new جديد
but he ولكنَّه • bad سيئ • well/good جيد

1- Complete the chart below with a suitable adjective for each of the pictures, as shown in the examples:

فاروق _____	يوسف _____	أمير _____	سمير سريع
مني _____	ليلي _____	سهير _____	كريمة سريعة
شادية _____ وجورج _____	سوسن _____ ونهى قبيحة	لاكي _____ وبونو كبير	كريم قصير وميمي طويلة

2- Can you work out the rule for changing the masculine word to the feminine one?

Write it down: _____

3- Now, match person to adjectives in the table below:

صغير وجميل	جميلة وطويلة	صغيرة وجميلة	بدين ووسيم	طويل ونحيف	adjectives
					name

4- Write down adjectives that describe the opposite of the following illustrations:

5 - Write down adjectives for the given illustrations as shown in the example:

محمد قصير و _____	الموتوسيكل جيد و _____	فاطمة صغيرة وجميلة
الصورة جميلة و _____	العلم _____ وجديد	المدينة _____ وجديدة

6- Write down the names of four actors and four actresses you know, using two adjectives to describe each one:

_____ و _____ : _____ ١-
_____ و _____ : _____ ٢-
_____ و _____ : _____ ٣-
_____ و _____ : _____ ٤-
_____ و _____ : _____ ٥-
_____ و _____ : _____ ٦-
_____ و _____ : _____ ٧-
_____ و _____ : _____ ٨-

Reflection:

Having completed this lesson, I know:

_____

I still have trouble with the following:

_____

_____

I still need to know more about the following:

_____

_____

Homework الواجب:

Now use the adjectives you wrote in sentences, following the example:

كريمة جميلة ولكنها سيئة   سامي صغير ولكنه طويل

_____   _____

_____   _____

_____   _____

_____   _____

_____   _____

Self assessment:

Having completed this lesson check what you can do:

1- I know and can easily write adjectives.   ( )

2- I can use adjectives when writing simple sentences.   ( )

3- I know the difference between masculine and feminine adjectives. ( )

الدرس الخامس

تسالي Entertainment

مراجعة Revision

Objectives:
Review of all previous lessons.

Useful Words

صغرى low • عظمى high • السعر price • البلاد countries
المدينة (ج) المُدُن city/cities • جنيه pound • هو he • هي she

---

1- You need to plan for your vacation. Your choice depends on several factors: the weather, the price, and the number of days available for your vacation. Look at the chart below, analyze it, and complete the chart on page 39 corresponding to cities and their temperatures:

درجة الحرارة Temperature		City
صغرى	عظمى	المدينة
		طابا
	٢٥	
٤		
	٤٣	
١٤		
		روما
	٤٢	
٨		
		الغردقة

2- You do not like hot weather, so write down the names of cities which you consider very hot in order to exclude them from your selection list:

_____

_____

3- Also write down the places that you have already visited, to shorten your selection list :

_____

_____

4- You need to know more about all the previous cities before deciding which one you will visit. Look again at the table and write down the name of the city that corresponds to the given country and the nationality of its citizens as shown in the example:

إيطاليّ / إيطاليَّة	روما	١ – إيطاليا
_____ / _____	_____	٢ – سوريا
_____ / _____	_____	٣ – اليمن
_____ / _____	_____	٤ – روسيا
_____ / إنجليزيّ	_____	٥ – إنجلترا
_____ / _____	_____	٦ – لبنان
_____ / _____	_____	٧ – الأردن
_____ / _____	_____	٨ – فرنسا
_____ / _____	_____	٩ – ألمانيا
_____ / _____	_____	١٠ – اليونان
_____ / _____	_____	١١ – قطر
_____ / _____	_____	١٢ – الإمارات
_____ / _____	_____	١٣ – الكويت
_____ / _____	_____	١٤ – السودان
_____ / _____	_____	١٥ – العراق

5- Write down the names of five countries and those of cities in those countries, then give them to your peer to match:

المدن	البلاد

6- In your search for the best price, you found the following trip costs. Look at them and complete the given table:

السعر price	عدد الأيام number of days	البلد country
		باريس وديزني
٥٩٠٠ جنيه		
	٤ أيام	
٧٧٠٠ جنيه		
	٩ أيام	
		قبرص
		باريس
٢٢٥٠ جنيه		

7- Once you decide which city you would like to visit, you need to take along some enjoyable games that you can play with your friends. Fill in the following table from 1 to 9 in such a way so as not to repeat the same number in any one horizontal or vertical line or in each 3x3 side square.

سودوكو Sudoku

٢			٣	٨	٦			١
	٩					٨	٢	
	٣	٧	١					
		٩		٢			٨	٧
١			٤		٧			٩
	٧		٨	١	٩	٦	٤	
٩	٨	٣	٢	٧	١	٤	٥	
	١	٦		٣		٧	٩	
				٦	٤			

8- Look at this year's calendar and write down five important dates that you want to remember, as shown in the example:

التاريخ the date	اليوم the day	المناسبة the occasion
٢٥ ديسمبر		الكريسماس
		الهالووين

9- One of the games which you played with your friends during your trip is "spin the bottle." One of the questions in the game is "describe the man of your dreams (فتى أحلامك) or the woman of your dreams (فتاة أحلامك)."

١- هي طويلة ونحيفة.

٢- هي ـــــــ و ـــــــ.

٣- هي ـــــــ و ـــــــ.

٤- ـــــــ و ـــــــ.

٥- ـــــــ و ـــــــ.

١- هو طويل ونحيف.

٢- هو ـــــــ و ـــــــ.

٣- هو ـــــــ و ـــــــ.

٤- ـــــــ و ـــــــ.

٥- ـــــــ و ـــــــ.

10- You spent a lot of money on your trip. So you decided to move to another, cheaper apartment with some of your friends. Consequently, you sent the following map to your friends in order to show them the apartment's location and the major spots around it.

a) Using this map of the building's floors, fill in the spaces on page 45 using the given adverbs of place:

Useful Words

the second floor الدور الثاني • the first floor الدور الأول
the street الشارع • the house البيت • the ground floor الدور الأرضي

الدور الثاني (2) (the second floor)

بيت المدير The manager's house	مكتب إيجار شُقَق An apartment estate agent's	معهد لغات A language institute

الدور الأول (1) (the first floor)

سوبر ماركت A supermarket	مكتبة A library	شقة الطلاب Student's hostel

الدور الأرضي (0) (the ground floor)

معمل A laboratory	عيادة دكتور A clinic	مخبز A bakery

between	بين
around	حول
far from	بعيد عن
on floor	في الدور
in front	أمام
beside	بجانب
above	فوق
behind	وراء
inside	في
below	تحت

١– شقة الطلاب _____ المكتبة.

٢– عيادة الدكتور _____ المكتبة.

٣– معهد اللغات _____ شقة الطلاب.

٤– المخبز _____ شقة الطلاب.

٥– السوبر ماركت _____ المعمل.

٦– مكتب الإيجار _____.

معهد اللغات وبيت المدير.

٧– المخبز _____ الدور الأول.

٨– المعمل _____ معهد اللغات.

b) Now provide the correct vocabulary items:

١– _____ بين _____ و _____.

٢– _____ تحت _____.

٣– _____ فوق _____.

٤– _____ بعيد عن _____.

٥– _____ قريب من _____.

٦– _____ بجانب _____.

c) From the vocabulary items on page 45 indicate where you could find the items illustrated below:

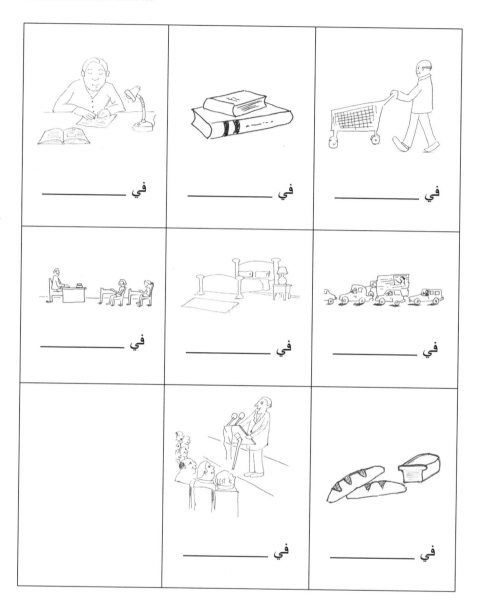

في _____   في _____   في _____

في _____   في _____   في _____

في _____   في _____

الوحدة الثانية

أنا والأسرة والأصدقاء

التعارف (١)

Getting Acquainted (1)

Objectives:

After completing this lesson, the students will be able to:

1- Introduce themselves to others.
2- Find out information about their peers.

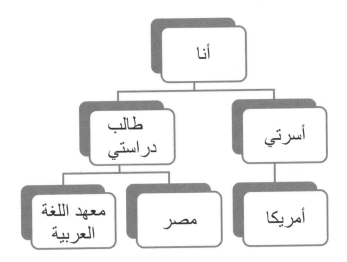

1- Look at the chart above and complete the following:

١. اسمي _____.

٢. أنا _____.

٣. أنا من _____.

٤. الآن أسكن في _____.

٥. أسرتي تسكن في _____.

٦. أدرس _____ في _____.

What extra information can you include about yourself (refer to the useful words):

٧. _____

٨. _____

٩. _____

١٠. _____

١١. _____

Useful Words

أدرس I study • أسكن I live • أحب I like • أنا اسمي My name
مدينة City • شارع Street • أسرتي My family
اللغة العربية the Arabic language • الآن Now • بيتي My home
التاريخ History • العلاقات الدولية International relations
الموسيقى Music • مِن From

2- Find out information about your colleagues and fill in the table below:

(Feel free to use the vocabulary provided in the tables below)

Dislikes لا أحب	Likes أحب	Countries visited البلاد التي زرتها	Study الدراسة	From which country البلد	Name الاسم

أمريكا • مصر • بريطانيا • لبنان • اليابان • فرنسا • ألمانيا • اللغة العربية
التاريخ • العلوم السياسية (political science) • العلاقات الدولية
دراسات الشرق الأوسط (Middle East Studies) • الأكل (eating)
الموسيقى • الناس (people) • الجامعة • بيتي • الصف • التسوق (shopping)
الدراسة (studying) • الازدحام (crowd) • التلوُّث (pollution)

3- Write down the information given in the following business card:

علي سيد أحمد
مدرس لغة عربية
جامعة القاهرة
العنوان: ٥٥ شارع المرعشلي–الزمالك– القاهرة
ت: ٢٧٣٥٩٣٥   فاكس: ٦٦٦٦٦٦
البريد الإلكتروني: ali@ali.com

الاسم: _____   العمل: _____
عنوان العمل : _____   الرقم: _____   الشارع: _____
الحي: _____   المدينة: _____
رقم التليفون: _____
رقم الفاكس: _____   البريد الإلكتروني: _____

Reflection:

Having completed this lesson, I know:

_____

_____

I still have trouble with the following:

_____

_____

I still need to know more about the following:

_____

_____

Homework الواجب :

1- Make your own business card:

2- Prepare some questions with which to interview your colleagues using the following guidelines, then check your questions' structure using the given checklist:

Question tools
with whom مَن مع • what ماذا • where أين • who مَن • what ما why ماذا • from where مِن أين • questions yes/no هل

Useful verbs:

You work = masc.: تعمل	fem.: تعملين	
You live = masc.: تسكن	fem.: تسكنين	
You study = masc.: تدرس	fem.: تدرسين	
You like = masc.: تحب	fem.: تحبين	

Checklist for questions:

- **Notice the word order in your questions:**

Question tool + verbal sentence, i.e.	ماذا تعمل ؟
Question tool + nominal sentence, i.e.	هل أنت طالب ؟
Question tool + a noun, i.e.	ما اسمك؟
Preposition + question tool + verbal sentence.	مع مَن تسكن؟
Question tool + prepositional phrase, i.e.	ماذا في البيت؟

- Appropriate suffix pronoun: i.e.,   ما اسمك ؟
- Appropriate verb conjugation: i.e.,   ماذا تعمل؟ / ماذا تعملون؟

/ ماذا تعملين ؟

Self assessment:

After completing this lesson, I can:

1- Introduce myself both orally and in writing.   (   )

2- Speak and write about my family, my studies, and places
   I have visited   (   )

3- Read information on business cards.   (   )

4- Ask others about themselves.   (   )

الدرس السابع
تعارف (٢)

Objectives:

After completing this lesson, the students will be able to:

1- Form questions according to the given statements.

2- Prepare for and undertake an interview.

Useful Words

you masc. أنتَ • you (fem.) أنتِ • no لا • yes نعم

your name (masc.) اسمكَ • your name (fem.) اسمكِ

you go to تذهب إلى • my friend (masc.) صديقي

1- Choose the correct question tool for the underlined answers:

١- أنا <u>من نيويورك</u>. (مَن – أين – مِن أين)

٢- أسرتي <u>في القاهرة</u>. (ماذا – أين – مع مَن)

٣- أدرس <u>العلاقات الدولية</u>. (ماذا– لماذا– أين)

٤- <u>نعم</u> أحب الموسيقى العربية. (ما– مِن أين – هل)

٥- <u>أنا كريم</u>. (مَن – ماذا– لماذا)

٦- هو يعمل <u>في البنك</u>. (ماذا – ما – أين)

٧- <u>كريمة</u> تدرس في الجامعة. (مَن – أين – ما)

٨- أسكن في <u>بيت الطلاب</u>. (مع مَن – مِن أين – أين)

٩- هو يسكن <u>مع الأسرة</u>. (مِن أين – لماذا – مع مَن)

١٠- <u>لا</u>، أنا لا أعمل. (هل – أين – ما)

2- Provide question tools:

١- ـ_____تدرس؟

التاريخ.

٢- ـ_____تحب الموسيقى الكلاسيكية؟

لا.

٣- ـ_____ تسكن؟

مع صديقي.

٤- ـ_____أنتِ لبنانية؟

نعم.

٥- ـ_____أنتَ؟

من فلوريدا.

٦- ـ_____تدرس؟

في القاهرة.

٧- ـ_____تسكن مع أسرتك؟

نعم.

٨- ـ_____ تعمل ؟

في الجامعة.

٩- ـ_____تسكن؟

في المعادي.

١٠- ـ_____ تحب في القاهرة؟

الأهرامات (pyramids).

3- Re-order the words to make questions:

١- أين – أنتَ – مِن : ـ_____؟

٢- تحب – هل – الموسيقى: ـ_____؟

٣- تسكن – مَن – مع: ـ_____؟

٤- تدرس– العلاقات الدولية – هل: ـ_____؟

٥- يحب – مَن – الموسيقى : ـ_____؟

٦- مصر – في – هل – تسكن: _____؟

٧- تذهب – الجامعة – إلى – لماذا _____؟

٨- تعمل – أين – الآن: _____؟

٩- البيت – ماذا – في : _____؟

١٠ – تدرس – ماذا – الجامعة – في: _____؟

4- Translate the following questions into Arabic, then answer them:

1- Who are you? _____

2- Where are you from? _____

3- What is your name? _____

4- Where do you live? _____

5- Are you a student? _____

6- Where do you work? _____

7- Do you like Arabic music? _____

8- Why do you study Arabic? _____

5- Write down the questions that correspond to the given answers:

١- _____؟

من مصر.

٢- _____؟

لا أنا لبنانية.

٣- _____؟

أعمل في بنك القاهرة.

٤- _____؟

نعم، أسكن في بيروت.

٥- _____؟

لا أنا أدرس في لبنان.

٦- _____؟

أسكن مع أسرتي.

٧- ــ؟

أدرس اللغة العربية في مصر.

٨- ــ؟

أحمد هو صديقي.

٩- ــ؟

هذه أسرتي.

١٠- ــ؟

نعم ، هي مصرية.

6- Now review with your colleague the questions which you prepared for the previous lessons homework.

7- Interview your colleague with these questions and try to take notes of the answers.

Reflection:

What I have discovered about forming questions in Arabic that is similar to my native language:

_____

_____

What I have discovered about forming questions in Arabic that is different from my native language:

_____

_____

I still have trouble with the following:

_____

_____

I still need to know more about the following:

_____

_____

Homework الواجب:

Write about your colleague from the information you got from him/her in class.

_____

_____

_____

Self assessment:

After completing this lesson I am able to:

1- Form questions using the correct word order.   (   )

2- Make sure I edit for gender agreement between verb and subject. (   )

الدرس الثامن

الأسرة

Objectives:

After completing this lesson students will be able to:

1- Write in more detail about their family members, using more verbs.
2- Use the adverb عند in their sentences.
3- Write a short paragraph using connectors.

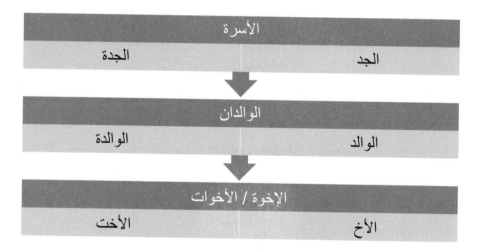

1- Look at the chart with your peer and try to work out the different members of the family:

Grandfather: _____ Grandmother: _____

Father: _____ Mother: _____ Parents: _____

Sisters: _____ Brothers: _____

Sister: _____ Brother: _____

2- Complete the following sentences:

١- والدي هو ــــــــــــــ.	هو يعمل في ــــــــــــــ.
٢- والدتي هي ــــــــــــــ.	هي تعمل في ــــــــــــــ.
٣- جدِّي في ــــــــــــــ.	هو لا ــــــــــــــ.
٤- جدتي في ــــــــــــــ.	جدتي اسمها ــــــــــــــ.
٥- عندي أخ. أخي اسمه ــــــــــــــ.	و يدرس ــــــــــــــ.
٦- أختي اسمها ــــــــــــــ.	هي طالبة في ــــــــــــــ.

3- Match the questions to the answers:

١- هل عندكَ أخ؟	– والدي يعمل في الجامعة
٢- ما اسم أختك؟	– لا، هي لا تعمل.
٣- أين يسكن جدك؟	– لا، ليس عندي إخوة
٤- هل والدتك مدرسة؟	– ليلى.
٥- هل عندك أسرة كبيرة؟	– جدي يسكن في المدينة.
٦- أين يعمل والدك؟	– نعم، جداً!!

4- Provide questions for the underlined part of the given answers:

١- ــــــــــــــــــــــــــــــــــــــ؟

نعم عندها أخت.

٢- ــــــــــــــــــــــــــــــــــــــ؟

لا، أختي مدرسة.

٣- _____؟

والدتي <u>طبيبة</u> .

٤- _____؟

لا، والدي <u>ليس عنده أخوات</u>.

٥- _____؟

نعم، <u>جدتي مصرية</u>.

٦- _____؟

<u>أختي اسمها سامية و هي تدرس في الجامعة</u>.

5- Look at the box below with the adverbial 'to have' conjugations and use it to complete the following questions:

١- يا جون، هل _____ أخ؟

٢- يا ليلى، هل _____ أخت؟

٣- هل والدتك _____ أخ يحب اللغة العربية؟

٤- هل جدك _____ بيت كبير؟

٥- هل _____ أخت تدرس في الجامعة يا ليلى؟

٦- من _____ أخوات؟

عندي I have/at my place • عندكَ you have (masc.) • عندكِ you have
(fem.) • عندَهُ he has • عندها she has • ليْسَ عندي I do not have

---

6- Write down some questions to ask your peer. Try to get more information about his/her family members using the verbs in the table below:

she lives تسكن • he lives يسكن • she works تعمل • he works يعمل she likes تحب • he likes يُحب • she studies تدرس • he studies يدرس he sleeps ينام • he cooksيطبخ • he reads يقرأ • he wants يريد he travelsيسافر • tries to يحاول أن • he graduates يتخرج

١– _____؟

٢ – _____؟

٣– _____؟

٤– _____؟

Illustratre all the information you obtained:

7- Now give the drawing to another peer to convert it to a paragraph about that person's family:

_____

_____

_____

_____

_____

8- Look at the illustration. You are one member of this family. Specify who you are, and write about your family members:

For each include:
الاسم – العمل – الدراسة
الصفات (descriptions)
– تاريخ الميلاد
يحب – تُحب – يحبون
يريد – تريد – يريدون

_____

_____

_____

_____

_____

9- Then try with your peer to read and to include connectors wherever suitable. Refer to the following list for connectors.

و • and • أيضاً also • ثم then • بالإضافة إلى ذلك in addition to that

Reflection:

Having completed this lesson, I know:

_____

_____

I still have trouble with the following:

_____

_____

I still need to know more about the following:

_____

_____

Homework الواجب :

1- You have a new Arab friend who does not read English. In order to get him to know more about you, write about members of your family in your Facebook profile. Include information about: Names, study, work, residence, likes, dislikes, descriptions.

2- Use the list of connectors on page 64.

_____

_____

_____

_____

_____

Self assessment:

Having completed this lesson, I am able to:

1- Write nominal sentences with agreement between subject and predicate in gender and number.   (   )

2- Use connectors to produce coherent paragraphs.   (   )

Objectives:

After completing this lesson the students will be able to:

1- Write down a dialogue.
2- Word Choice more information from peers.
3- Change a dialogue into a paragraph.
4- Write comparisons using suitable connectors.

From now on write the date in each lesson as shown in the example:

الأحد، ١٠ يونيه ٢٠١٢

التاريخ (the date): _____

Useful Words

الأصدقاء friends • أصدقائي my friends • وسط المدينة downtown
السفر traveling • موظف an employee • شركة a company

1- It is the first time you meet كريمة. Use the given information to complete the dialogue with her:

القاهرة   مصر   جامعة القاهرة   اللغة الأسبانية   كريمة

١- _____؟

كريمة.

٢- هل تعملين في القاهرة؟

_____

٣- _____؟

في جامعة القاهرة.

٤- _____؟

نعم أنا مصرية.

٥- أين تسكنين؟

_____

2- Now write down what you know about كريمة

_____

_____

_____

_____

3- Add extra information of your choice:

_____

_____

4- Now use the following information about سامي to complete the following dialogue with him:

لبنان   وسـط المدينة   موظف   الجامعة العربية   سـامي

١- هل أنت أحمد؟

_____.

٢- _____؟

لا، أنا أعمل.

٣- أين تعمل؟

_____.

٤- _____؟

في وسط المدينة.

٥- هل أنت مصري؟

_____.

5- Now write what you know about سامي :

_____

_____

_____

_____

6- Add extra information of your choice:

_____

_____

7- Complete the sentences following the example, then write your own:

١- كريمة من مصر لكن سامي من لبنان.

٢- _____ لكن كريمة لا تعمل.

٣- هي طالبة _____.

٤- _____.

٥- _____.

٦- _____.

8- a) Look at the information about أحمـد and complete the map in the same way about two more of your friends (masculine and feminine):

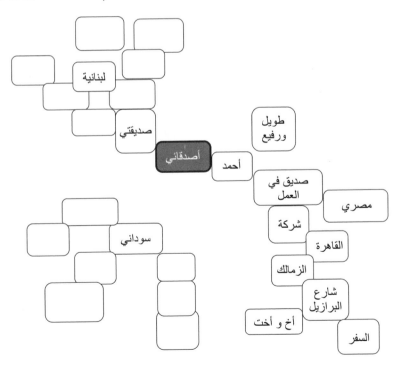

b) Fill in the following table with common and different information about your three friends, as shown in the example.

صديقي	صديقتي	أحمد
هو سوداني	هي لبنانية	هو مصري

c) Transfer information into paragraphs about each one:

أحمد: _____

_____

_____

_____

_____

_____

صديقتي: _____

_____

_____

_____

_____

صديقي: _____

_____

_____

_____

_____

9- Now use the information in the paragraphs to make a dialogue between the three friends when they meet each other for the first time:

_____

_____

_____

_____

_____

_____

_____

_____

_____

Reflection:

Having completed this lesson, I know:

_____

_____

I still have trouble with the following:

_____

_____

I still need to know more about the following:

_____

_____

Homework الواجب :

In an attempt to know more about your friends, write one paragraph in your diary which shows common and different information about Ahmed and your other two friends. Do not forget to use the connectors which you learnt previously.

و • أيضاً • بالإضافة إلى ذلك • ثم • لكن • إنما

Self assessment:

Having completed this lesson, I am able to :

1- Change a dialogue into a paragraph.   (   )

2- Change a paragraph into a dialogue.   (   )

3- Compare between sentences using the correct connectors.   (   )

4- Edit for gender agreement whenever I write.   (   )

5- To conjugate some verbs with some nouns or pronouns.   (   )

الدرس العاشر

الصفات (٢)

Objectives:

After completing this lesson, the students will know how to:

1- Write down parts of the body.
2- Write adjectives and nouns to describe people.
3- Use connectors to compare people.

التاريخ : _____

Useful Words

نظارة eyeglasses • جسم الإنسان human body • جداً very • وجه face
أسنان teeth • رأس head • شارب a mustache • مكسورة broken
واسع wide • ضيق narrow • الرقص dancing • القراءة reading
السفر traveling • نشيط active • هادئ quiet • خجول shy
يلبس=he wears • أما....ف ...as for • خجول shy

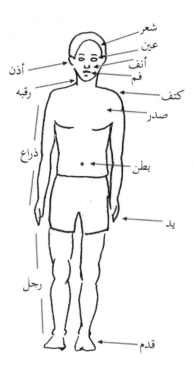

شعر
عين
أنف
أذن — فم
رقبه — كتف
صدر
ذراع — بطن

يد

رجل

قدم

1- You saw a thief running out of your neighbor's apartment. You described the thief as follows. Your colleague will read the information provided and draw a picture of the thief:

١- الوجه : طويل

٢- العين : واسعة

٣- الأنف :كبير

٤- الأذن : صغيرة

٥- الشعر: قصير جداً

٦- الشارب : رفيع

٧- الفم : واسع

٨- الأسنان : مكسورة

2- Now use the information given to describe him in sentences. Hint: do not forget to include possessive pronouns like (وجهه طويل):

_____

_____

_____

_____

3- Another person has seen the thief, but described him in exactly the opposite way. Write down his description:

_____

_____

_____

_____

4- Look at the previous picture and complete the following sentences accordingly. You will know the names of each person in the picture by the number beside his/her name:

(١) أشرف / (٢) كريم / (٣) محمود / (٤) أماني / (٥) كمال / (٦) هدى / (٧) أحمد / (٨) سمير / (٩) ليلى / (١٠) علي / (١١) سميرة

> - Use previous adjectives, in addition to the Useful Words list :
>
> طويل / قصير / رفيع / بدين = سمين / كبير / صغير
>
> - Remember the gender agreement between nouns and adjectives

– أحمد _____ وطويل.

– سميرة شعرها _____ وهدى أيضاً.

– محمود _____ وشعره قصير.

– سمير يلبس _____ وكمال أيضاً.

– اشرف أنفه _____.

– _____ بدينة.

– أحمد لا _____ نظارة.

– علي شعره _____.

– أشرف أذنه (fem. word) _____.

– ليلى نشيطة جداً و_____ أيضاً.

– _____ مدرس موسيقى.

– _____ تحب الرقص.

– هدى خجولة و_____.

– كمال شعره _____.

– محمود عنده _____.

– علي يحب _____ والكتب.

– سمير يحب _____.

– كمال ليس _____ وليس بديناً.

5- Use ...ف ...أما ...to compare between some of the people, as in the example:

أحمد طويل وشعره قصير أما كمال فقصير ويلبس نظارة.

‏١-_____

‏٢-_____

‏٣-_____

‏٤-_____

‏٥-_____

Reflection:

Having completed this lesson, I know:

_____

_____

I still have trouble with the following:

_____

_____

I still need to know more about the following:

_____

_____

Homework الواجب:

Create a family album, describing family members and friends, using adjectives and ...ف ...أما ... (do not forget to edit for agreement).

Self Assessment:

Having completed this lesson, I can do the following:

1- Write a number of adjectives. ( )

2- Differentiate between masculine and feminine adjectives easily. ( )

3- Describe people and things using adjectives. ( )

4- Be aware of agreement between masculine and feminine nouns
and adjectives. ( )

5- Write paragraphs comparing between descriptions. ( )

الدرس الحادي عشر

أنا والأسرة والأصدقاء (مراجعة)

Objectives:
Review some of the previous items.

التاريخ : _____

Useful Words

مُنْذُ for/since • الآن now • الهندسة engineering
ستتخرج you will graduate • شركة a company • سنة a year
سنتين two years • الأسبوع الماضي last week

1- Complete the following sentences using منذ – الآن :

١- أنا أدرس اللغة العربية _____ سنتين.

٢- والدي يعمل في القاهرة _____ .

٣- أنتَ تسكن في مصر _____ شهر.

٤- _____ أنا أعمل في شركة كبيرة.

٥- أختي تدرس الهندسة _____ سنة.

2- Choose one word from every column to make correct sentences :

الآن	في	يعمل	تسكن	عندي أخ
مهندساً	القاهرة	في الجامعة الأمريكية	عنده أخ	والدتي
واشنطون	مُنذ	الهندسة	يحب	أختي
سنة	ويعمل	في مدينة	تدرس	والدي

_____ ١-

_____ ٢-

_____ ٣-

_____ ٤-

3-Provide different question words, then answer the questions:

._____ عندكَ أخ؟ _____ ١-

._____ يعمل والدك؟ _____ ٢-

._____ تعمل والدتك؟ _____ ٣-

._____ اسم أختك؟ _____ ٤-

._____ تسكن؟ _____ ٥-

4- Match opposites, then use in sentences:

– تحت	١- والد
– منذ شهر	٢- أخ
– والدة	٣- الآن
– أخت	٤- جدي
– صغير	٥- فوق
– جدتي	٦- كبير

_____ ١-

_____ ٢-

_____ ٣-

_____ ٤-

_____ ٥-

_____ ٦-

5-Circle the correct answer, then write it in a sentence adding more information.

١- أين يعمل والدك؟

أ- منذ سنة   ب- في الجامعة   ج- اسمه أحمد

_____

٢- ماذا تدرس أختك؟

أ- الزمالك   ب- سنتين   ج- الهندسة

_____

٣- هل تعمل والدتك؟

أ- لا، هو لا يعمل   ب- الآن   ج- نعم، في شركة

_____

٤ - أين تسكن؟

أ- في المطعم   ب- في السوبر ماركت   ج- في المدينة

_____

٥ - متى ستتخرج من الجامعة؟

أ- منذ شهر   ب- بعد سنة   ج- الأسبوع الماضي

_____

6- Choose sentences from all previous drills, and write a paragraph entitled " أنا وأسرتي ". Write as much information as you can. Do not forget to use the following connectors:

و • أيضاً • ثم – بالإضافة إلى ذلك – لكن • إنما • أما.....ف

_____

_____

_____

_____

_____

Homework الواجب:

You have not heard from one of your childhood friends for a long time. Write a paragraph in your diary to describe him/her as much as you can.

الوحدة الثالثة

أنا وبيتى وشارعي

الدرس الثاني عشر

بيتي (١)

Objectives:

After completing this lesson, students will know the following:

1- Names of rooms in the house.
2- Names of some furniture items.
3- How to construct nominal sentences with up-fronted predicates.
4- How to extend sentences.
5- Some important collocations.

التاريخ : _____

Useful Words

he sits يجلس • he bathes يستحم • he eats the food يتناول الطعام
يطبخ he cooks • ينام he sleeps - جانبي side • رئيسي main
wide واسع • near قريب • far بعيد • expensive غالية • cheap رخيص
the apartment الشقة • comfortable مريح • crowded مزدحم
the club النادي • an area منطقة • rent إيجار • advertisement إعلان
how much(price)? بكم/how many/much? كم
a lot كثيراً • a little قليلاً • international relations العلاقات الدولية
porter بوّاب • schools مدرسة/مدارس • cars سيارة/سيارات
people ناس • neighbors جار/جيران

1- a) Match verbs with names of rooms.
   b) Write names of rooms provided under each picture:

– نام/ينام – تناول الطعام/يتناول الطعام – طبخ/يطبخ

استحم/يستحم – جلس/يجلس

Names of rooms:

المطبخ – غرفة الجلوس – غرفة النوم – غرفة الطعام – الحمّام

2- Now write down the name of each object in this table under the room where it belongs on page 88:

سرير	ثلاجة	تواليت
شباك	طاولة	خزانة
فنجان	مكتبة	كرسي
سكين	ملعقة	حوض
بانيو	مكتب	كنبة
نور	طبق	تلفزيون
شوكة	سخَّان	بوتاجاز

الحمام	المطبخ	غرفة الطعام	غرفة الجلوس	غرفة النوم
————	————	————	————	————
————	———·——	————	————	————
————	————	————	————	————
————	————	————	————	————

3- Write sentences using the above objects as shown in the example. Be sure to add adjectives:

في غرفة النوم سرير كبير

_____ -٢	_____ -١
_____ -٤	_____ -٣
_____ -٦	_____ -٥
_____ -٨	_____ -٧
_____ -١٠	_____ -٩

4- Read the following passage, then answer the questions:

أنا خالد، أنا من الكويت وأدرس العلاقات الدولية في جامعة الإسكندرية. أسكن في منطقة جميلة، لكنها بعيدة قليلاً عن الجامعة. بيتي في شارع جانبي، لكنّه مزدحم جداً. شقتي في الدور الأول، هي صغيرة لكنها مريحة. في شقتي غرفة نوم واحدة، لكنها واسعة. الحمام في بيتي صغير، لكن المطبخ واسع وكبير وعلى الشارع. أنا أحب بيتي كثيراً.

a) Pair work : Choose from the given vocabulary to add extra information wherever possible in the previous passage:

سيارة / سيارات – مكتب/ مكاتب – شارع / شوارع – مدرسة / مدارس – بنك – مكتبة – سوبر ماركِت

بوَّاب – جار /جيران – ناس – أسرتي – الإيجار غالٍ/رخيص – الباص – المترو – التاكسي / التاكسيات

Adverbs of place : فوقَ – تحتَ – أمام – خلف – بجانب – عند – في

_____

_____

_____

_____

b) Write a dialogue with خالد about his apartment:

أنت: _____

خالد: _____

أنت: _____

خالد: _____

أنت: _____

خالد: _____

5- Complete sentences to compare between your apartment and شقة خالد:

١– شقة خالد صغيرة لكن شقتي _____ .

٢– شقة خالد فيها غرفة واحدة _____ .

٣– شقة خالد على الشارع _____ .

٤– شقتي فيها ٣ حمامات _____ .

٥– شقتي في القاهرة ولكن شقة خالد ف_____ .

٦– شقة خالد في شارع جانبي_____ .

٧–_____ .

٨–_____ .

6- Choose collocations that describe the given words:

١- شارع : طويل – قصير – صغير – كبير – جانبي – رخيص

٢- مدينة : بعيدة – طويلة – صغيرة – رئيسية – قريبة – رخيصة

٣- شقة : بعيدة – قصيرة – واسعة – غالية – كبيرة – مزدحمة

٤- منطقة : غالية – طويلة – بعيدة – جانبية – جميلة – كبيرة

٥- غرفة : قصيرة – غالية – مريحة – صغيرة – واسعة – بعيدة

7- Now use what you have learned in this lesson to write a paragraph describing your house back home:

_____

_____

_____

_____

_____

_____

_____

_____

Reflection:

Having completed this lesson, I know:

_____

_____

I still have trouble with the following:

_____

_____

I still need to know more about the following:

_____

_____

Homework الواجب :

You want to rent your apartment for the summer. Write an advertisement for the newspaper, describing it (remember advertisements are expensive):

```




```

Self assessment:

Having completed this lesson I know:

1- Vocabulary of rooms in the house.   ( )

2- Vocabulary of different furniture items.   ( )

3- How to construct up-fronted predicate sentences.   ( )

4- How to add more details to sentences.   ( )

5- How to construct some collocations.   ( )

الدرس الثالث عشر

بيتي (٢)

Objectives:

After completing this lesson, students will be able to:

1- Use 'at home' vocabulary to write questions, word choice, and paragraphs.
2- Compare using different tools.

التاريخ : _____

1- Read the following passage and write questions. Be sure to include adjectives and/or adverbs:

في بيتي غرفة نوم كبيرة فيها سرير وخزانة، وغرفة جلوس جميلة لها بلكون صغير على حديقة وفيها كنبة مريحة وكراسي جديدة إلى جانب مكتبة فيها كتب كثيرة، هناك أيضاً غرفة طعام فيها طاولة كبيرة وكراسي كثيرة وشباك كبير على شارع مزدحم بالسيارات، وهي بجانب المطبخ الذي فيه ثلاجة جديدة وبوتاجاز قديم لا يعمل جيداً. في البيت هناك حمام واحد فقط، ولكن كبير ونظيف. أنا أحب بيتي كثيراً لأن عندي جيران ممتازين وأيضاً لأن إيجاره رخيص!

١- _____؟

٢- _____؟

٣- _____؟

٤- _____؟

٥- _____؟

2- Now write down other similar questions to ask your peer about his apartment, and then write a paragraph describing it:

a- Questions:

١– ـــ ؟

٢– ـــ ؟

٣– ـــ ؟

٤– ـــ ؟

٥– ـــ ؟

b- Description:

ـــ

ـــ

ـــ

ـــ

ـــ

ـــ

ـــ

ـــ

3- You want to sell your apartment, Give descriptions that are opposite to the true ones provided:

Remember:

كثير • قليل • كبير • صغير • جميل • قبيح • جديد • قديم • قريب • بعيد

غالٍ • رخيص • واسع • ضيق (narrow) • نظيف (clean)

١– الشقة ضيقة وإيجارها غالٍ: ـــ

٢– غرفة النوم صغيرة والسرير مُتعِب : ـــــــــــــــــــــــــــــــــــــ

٣– في المطبخ شباك صغير جداً: ـــ

٤– الكنبة والكراسي كلها قديمة: ـــ

٥– الحمام ضيق وغير نظيف: _____

٦– ليس فيها بلكونات: _____

٧– غرفة الطعام بعيدة عن المطبخ: _____

٨– الشقة على شارع قبيح وغير نظيف: _____

4- Look at the examples below. What do you think is their function? Underline the connectors that made this clear.

١– المطبخ واسع أما الحمام فضيق.

٢– غرفة النوم كبيرة أما غرفة الجلوس فصغيرة.

٣– بيتي في أمريكا غالٍ أما بيتي في مصر فرخيص.

٤– السرير مريح ولكن الكنبة غير مريحة.

٥– الغرف واسعة ولكن المطبخ ضيق.

٦–التلفزيون جديد ولكن الكومبيوتر قديم.

٧– الحمام واسع وكذلك المطبخ.

٨– السرير مريح والكنبة كذلك.

٩– الكراسي جديدة و كذلك الطاولة.

١٠– بيتي رخيص ومريح أيضاً.

١١– الحمام نظيف و المطبخ أيضاً.

١٢– البلكونة كبيرة و الشباك أيضاً.

Connector	Function

5- Now compare your peer's apartment with your own. Be sure to use the above connectors:

_____
_____
_____
_____
_____
_____
_____
_____

6- Try to guess the meaning of the underlined words after relating them to adjectives you know:

شقة (١) أكبر من شقة (٢)

شقة (١) أغلى من شقة (٢)

الغرف في شقة (١) أكثر من الغرف في شقة (٢)

What is the preposition used with it?
Does it have a function?

Notes:

_____

7- Use this structure, as well as the following connectors to compare and contrast your apartment in Egypt with that in your country:

– ..أما ... فـ...	١- _____
– و لكنْ ...	٢- _____
– وكذلك / كذلك	٣- _____
– أيضاً	٤- _____
	٥- _____
	٦- _____

Reflection:

Having completed this lesson, I know:

_____

_____

I still have trouble with the following:

_____

_____

I still need to know more about the following:

_____

_____

Homework الواجب:

Now write about your dream house. Feel free to use the previous connectors and structures, and some of the given vocabulary:

swimming pool حمام سباحة	_____
garden حديقة	_____
on the mountain على الجبل	_____
in the countryside في الريف	_____
in the city في المدينة	_____
tennis court ملعب تنس	_____
gym صالة رياضة	_____
football pitch ملعب كرة	_____

Self assessment:

Having completed this lesson, I am able to do the following:

1- Write a paragraph about my home.   (   )

2- Use connectors to show similarities and differences.   (   )

3- Edit for agreement.   (   )

الدرس الرابع عشر
في الشارع

Objectives:

After completing this lesson, students will be able to do the following:

1- Identify new vocabulary items using a guessing strategy.
2- Describe a place using senses.
3- Use adverbs of place correctly.
4- Ensure agreement between nonhuman plurals and feminine
   singular adjectives.

التاريخ : ـــــــــــــــــــــــــــــــــ

1-Read the following passage and identify places in the street from the pictures on page 98:

بيتي في شارع القصر العيني، هذا شارع رئيسي ومزدحم وفيه سيارات وباصات كثيرة طوال النهار والليل، كما أنَّ فيه محال كثيرة أيضاً، فبالقرب من بيتي هناك محطة بنزين، وجزار ومحل عصير مشهور إلى جانب مقهى شعبي يقدم الشيشة والسحلب وأغاني أم كلثوم من الراديو الذي على الحائط. على الجانب الآخر من الرصيف، هناك مكتبة كبيرة فيها كتب عربية وأجنبية وبجانبها سوق مزدحم للخضر والفاكهة الطازجة دائماً، وفي أول الشارع هناك جراج للسيارات وأمامه عمارة كلها أطباء وتحتها صيدلية جديدة، أما تحت بيتي، فهناك سوبر ماركت صغير ولكن فيه كل ما أحتاج إليه وحلاق أذهب إليه مرة كل شهر . هناك أيضاً مطاعم صغيرة وكثيرة في هذا الشارع، فهناك مطعم للشاورمة وآخر للفول والطعمية إلى جانب مطعم آخر للكشري وآخر غالٍ للكباب والكفتة. أنا أحب أن آكل كل يوم في مطعم مختلف، ولا أشعر بالوحدة أبداً لأني دائماً أتكلم مع ناس كثيرين في هذا الشارع، لذلك أحب السكن في هذه المنطقة.

2- Now draw that street:

（空白框）

3- Underline all items found in the given places, Follow the example:

١- في المقهى: (شاي – شيشة – لحم – دواء – خضر)

٢- في الصيدلية: (سيارات – كتب – دواء – قطن – فاكهة – شامبو)

٣- عند الجزار: (شاورمة – كشري – كفتة – دواء – شيشة – فاكهة)

٤- في المكتبة (دواء – دجاج – بنزين – كتب عربية – قهوة – جريدة)

٥- في محطة البنزين: (قهوة – سيارات – عُمال – مطعم – سحلب – كتب)

٦- في المطعم: (خضر – شيشة – دواء – فاكهة – لحم – شاورمة – كشري)

4- Look back to the passage and underline all connectors. Discuss their function with your peer, and then discuss them with all the class, giving examples of your own:

_____

_____

_____

_____

5- Write sentences from the above passage that show the following:

a- Things he sees in the street:

_____

_____

b- Things he hears in the street:

_____

_____

c- Things he smells in the street:

_____

_____

d- Things he touches in the street:

_____

_____

e- Things he tastes in the street:

_____

_____

6- Write down questions to ask your peer about the street he lives in (write down the answers):

١- _____ ؟

٢- _____ ؟

٣- _____ ؟

٤- _____ ؟

٥- _____ ؟

٦- _____ ؟

7- Now describe the street you have been asking about:

_____

_____

_____

_____

_____

_____

_____

8- This is the street on which I live. Look at the pictures and describe it, using the given connectors:

في وسط الشارع • بجانب • في آخر الشارع • بين • أمام • خلف • بالقرب من •
بعيد عن • إلى جانبه • في أول الشارع • عند • إلى يمين • إلى يسار

_____

_____

_____

_____

_____

_____

_____

_____

_____

_____

Reflection:

Having completed this lesson, I know:

_____

_____

I still have trouble with the following:

_____

_____

I still need to know more about the following:

_____

_____

Homework الواجب:

Describe a street in your city. Be sure to include different places where senses could play a role (that is where you see things, taste things, smell things, hear sounds, and talk to people), as well as adverbs of place.

Remember these adverbs:
في أول • في آخر بالقرب من • بعيد عن هنا • هناك • بجانب فوق • تحت • أمام • خلف • عند

_____

_____

_____

_____

_____

_____

Self assessment:

Having completed this lesson I am able to do the following:

1- Use senses in describing a place.   ( )

2- Use adverbs of place in describing a place.   ( )

3- Guess meanings of new words from words I already know.   ( )

4- Edit for agreement between nonhuman plurals and feminie

    singular adjectives.   ( )

5- Understand and write names of different shops.   ( )

الوحدة الرابعة

ماذا أفعل وماذا فعلت وماذا كنت أفعل؟

الدرس الخامس عشر

يوم الإجازة

Objectives:

After completing this lesson, students will know how to:

1- Use a guessing strategy to learn new verbs and vocabulary items.
2- Use the present tense to describe actions taking place in the habitual order.

التاريخ : _____

في يوم الإجازة أصحو من النوم متأخراً، في الساعة العاشرة، وبعد ذلك أدخل الحمام وآخذ دشاً بارداً ثم أعمل كوباً من الشاي وسندوتش جبن أبيض بالطماطم. في أثناء ذلك أستمع إلى الراديو أو أقرأ الجريدة وأحياناً أفكر فيما سأفعل هذا اليوم. بعد أن آكل، أنزل إلى السوبر ماركت الذي تحت البيت لأشتري طعام الأسبوع كله مرة واحدة. في الساعة الثانية عشرة اتصل بأصدقائي وعادةً نخرج معاً. أحياناً نذهب إلى السينما، أو نتمشَّى في المراكز التجارية الكبيرة، وأحياناً أخرى نأخذ مركباً في النيل أو نركب عجلاً في الشوارع الهادئة. في المساء نذهب لنأكل في أي مطعم من المطاعم الموجودة بجانب بيتي ثم نشاهد التلفزيون أو نلعب كوتشينة في منزل أحدنا. وعندما يأتي الليل، أكون مُتعباً جداً فأنام تقريباً في الساعة الحادية عشرة لأستعد ليوم الإجازة التالي.

1- Read the passage on page 107 and complete the following table with the verbs from the passage then guess their meaning from the context:

Verb	Meaning

2- Use an appropriate verb from the list on page 108 then complete the sentence:

١- كل يوم في الصباح _____.

٢- عندما تأتي الإجازة _____.

٣- في المطعم _____.

٤- أخرج من بيتي لـ _____.

٥- كل يوم بعد أن أصحو _____.

٦- أحب أنْ _____.

٧- من اللازم أنْ _____.

٨- هل من الممكن أنْ _____؟

3- Complete the following sentences according to the pictures, then put them in a suitable sequence:

هو يشاهد _____ .

يصحو من النوم _____ .

هو يعمل _____ .

يحب أن _____ .

يأكل _____ .

من اللازم أنْ _____ .

يحب أن يدرس _____ .

ينام وهو _____ .

4- Now use the above sentences in a dialogue between you and the person in the pictures, asking him about his daily routine (ask for extra details):

_____ ؟

_____ ؟

_____ ؟

_____ ؟

_____ ؟

_____ ؟

5- Use each group of verbs to write about the person in the illustration:

١- يأكل – يشرب – يشاهد – يحب أنْ

_____

_____

_____

٢- من اللازم أنْ – يقرأ – يأخذ – يعمل

_____

_____

_____

_____

٣- تستمع إلى – تفكر – تحب – تتصل

_____

_____

_____

_____

_____

٤- يحب أنْ ْ – يطبخ – يشتري – يستعدّ

_____

_____

_____

_____

_____

٥- تتصل – تخرج – تذهب – تتمشّى

_____

_____

_____

_____

6- Look at the illustration below and write down what you want to do this summer (use as many verbs as you can, as well as connectors):

New Verbs	
To travel يسافر	في الصباح – في المساء– في وقت الظهر – بعد الظهر – في الليل – وبعد ذلك – ثم – لـ + فعل مضارع – أولاً – و أخيراً – كل يوم – يوم الإجازة – وفي الساعة ...
To visit يزور	
To see يرى	
To stay يبقَى	

_____

_____

_____

_____

_____

_____

_____

_____

_____

_____

Reflection:

Having completed this lesson, I know:

_____

_____

I still have trouble with the following:

_____

_____

I still need to know more about the following:

_____

_____

Homework الـواجـب:

Write a paragrah about things that you have to do everyday which you do not like

In class, before writing:

a- Brainstorm with your peer the verbs that you are going to use, as well as some necessary connectors.

_____

_____

_____

_____

b- Each group writes on the board what they have chosen.

c- Take notes of what the others wrote.

_____

_____

_____

_____

d- Consult the teacher for new words.

_____

_____

_____

_____

Self assessment:

Having completed this lesson, I am able to:

1- Use the correct verbs for writing about habitual actions. ( )

2- Conjugate verbs for different persons. ( )

3- Use connectors to produce a coherent narration. ( )

4- Use verbs that take أنْ properly. ( )

5- Use adverbs of time to connect sentences. ( )

أمس في المطعم

Objectives:
After completing this lesson, students will be able to:

1- Write sentences in the past tense.
2- Conjugate verbs for singular first and third persons in the past tense.
3- Change sentences into a paragraph using connectors.
4- Be acquainted with some collocations.

التاريخ : _____

1- Write down with your peer as many past tense verbs about going to a restaurant:

_____

_____

_____

2- Use vocabulary in boxes 1 and 2 on page 116 to make sentences about each illustration:

٢		١		
عامل المطعم	المطعم	أنا	هي	هو
طبق اليوم	صديقي/صديقتي	ذهبتُ	ذهبَتْ	ذهبَ
الجريدة	شاي/قهوة/عصير	قابلتُ	قابَلَتْ	قابلَ
العمل / الرحلة / الدراسة		تناولْتُ	تناولَتْ	تناوَلَ
تذكرة سينما	كتاب جديد	شَرِبْتُ	شَرِبَتْ	شربَ
باص	سيارة أجرة	تكلمتُ مع	تكلَّمَتْ مع	تكلَّمَ مع
الجامعة	البيت	مشيتُ	مشيَتْ	مشي
السوق	المكتب	اشتريتُ	اشترَتْ	اشترى

٣	
ثم/ ف / وبعد ذلك / و / أخيراً / وعندما /	رَكِبْتُ ← رَكِبَتْ ← ركبَ
/ ولكن / و بسبب	رجعْتُ ← رَجعَتْ ← رجعَ
لأنَّ / الذي	

| ٧ | ٨ | ٩ |

١- _____ ؟

٢- _____ ؟

٣- _____ ؟

٤- _____ ؟

٥- _____ ؟

٦- _____ ؟

٧- _____ ؟

٨- _____ ؟

٩- _____ ؟

3- Now write a story about Ahmad and Layla, using the same pictures, in any sequence you like, and using connectors from box 3 on page 116 (be sure to use correct verb conjugation):

_____

_____

_____

_____

_____

_____

_____

_____

_____

4- Write down the verb(s) that would make sense with the following nouns:

١- قهوة : _____

٢- الغداء: _____

٣- كتاب جديد: _____

٤- السوق : _____

٥- الباص: _____

٦- الشرق الأوسط: _____

٧- بلده: _____

٨- الأصدقاء: _____

5- Answer the questions below, then use answers and connectors in the box to write a paragraph:

أخيراً	بعد قليل	كثيراً	لكن	ثُمَّ	بعد ذلك	فَ	لِ

١- أين ذهبت أمس؟ _____

٢- لماذا ذهبت هناك؟ _____

٣- ماذا رأيت هناك؟ _____

٤- أين جلست؟ _____

٥- ماذا شربت؟ وماذا أكلت؟ _____

٦- هل رأيت أصدقاءك؟ _____

٧- هل تكلمت معهم؟ _____

٨- ماذا قرأت هناك؟ وماذا كتبت؟ _____

٩- كيف رجعت إلى البيت بعد ذلك؟ _____

۱۰-كيف كانت محطة الباص ؟ _____
_____
۱۱- متى رجعت إلى البيت؟ _____
_____
۱۲- بماذا شعرت ؟ _____
_____
۱۳- ماذا فعلت في البيت؟ _____
_____
۱٤- ماذا تريد أن تفعل غداً؟ _____
_____

Reflection:

Having completed this lesson, I know:

_____

_____

I still have trouble with the following:

_____

_____

I still need to know more about the following:

_____

_____

Homework الـواجـب:

Answer the questions in a paragraph (use the connectors provided):

ماذا فعلت في الإجازة؟

أنا ذهبتُ إلى (أين؟)   (متى؟)   (مع من؟) (لماذا؟) ، وهناك:

رأيتُ _____

سمعتُ _____

تكلمتُ مع _____

شربتُ _____

أكلتُ _____

تمشَّيت في _____

اشتريتُ _____

شعرتُ بـ _____

نمتُ _____

ثم • وبعد ذلك • لأنني • وعندما • ولكن • فـ • وبعد قليل • في الساعة العاشرة •
وقت الظهر • يوم الجمعة الماضي • وأخيراً

_____

_____

_____

_____

_____

_____

_____

_____

_____

Self assessment:

Having completed this lesson, I am able to:

1-Narrate in the past.   (   )

2- Use connectors to create a cohesive and coherent text from

   separate sentences.   (   )

3- Use collocations in writing.   (   )

4- Conjugate verbs in the past for the first and third singular persons.   (   )

الدرس السابع عشر

اسمها ليلى

Objectives:

1- Read an authentic text and start analyzing its structures.
2- Construct sentences with different structures.
3- Construct sentences with different tenses.
4- Use more connectors between sentences.

التاريخ : ــــــــــــــــــــــــــــــــــــ

Pre-reading activity : نشاط ما قبل القراءة

١. مع من تعيش؟ ـــــــــــــــــــــــــــــــ

٢. أين تعيش؟ ـــــــــــــــــــــــــــــــــ

٣. ماذا تفعل كل يوم؟ ــــــــــــــــــــــــــ

٤. في مجموعات، اكتبوا بعض الأفعال الأخرى المتعلقة بالنشاط اليومي في المربع.

Read the following article, then answer the questions:

صندوق الدنيا
بقلم : أحمد بهجت (بتصرف)
٢٠٠٤/٩/٢
اسمها ليلى
طفلة عمرها سبع سنوات...

١. كانت تعيش مع والدها ووالدتها وأختها وأخيها وجدتها العجوز. كانت ليلى تقضي وقتها في اللعب. وفجأة مات الأب والأم في حادث، فوجدت ليلى نفسها تواجه مشكلة.

٢. فجدتها العجوز تتحرك بصعوبة. وشقيقتها تبلغ الرابعة من عمرها. أما شقيقها الصغير فيبلغ الثانية من عمره.

٣. كل يوم تستيقظ ليلى من نومها , فتعد طعام الإفطار لجدتها العجوز وشقيقتها وشقيقها. وبعد ذلك ترتب البيت بسرعة ثم تسرع إلي الشارع وتذهب إلى المدرسة.

٤. بعد أن تخرج من المدرسة تمر على السوق, ثم تعود إلى البيت فتعد الطعام وتذاكر دروسها.

٥. وهكذا كانت المسؤولية كبيرة على الطفلة الصغيرة. ولكنها لا تشكو بل تطيل ساعات يومها وتقلل ساعات نومها لتخدم الأسرة.

٦. وخلال هذا الكفاح اليومي لا تنسى ليلى أن تتحدث مع جدتها وتلعب مع شقيقها وتدرس شقيقتها، وأكثر من ذلك، لا تنسى ليلى بسمتها مع الجميع.

٧. وما زال الوقت يضيق ويمضي, ومازالت المسؤولية تزيد، ومازالت ليلى صامدة تتحمل المسؤولية بكل شجاعة وصبر.

To live	عاش، يعيش
To die	مات، يموت
To spend time	قضى، يقضي (وقت)
Suddenly	فجأة
To face	واجه، يواجه
To move	تحرّك، يتحرك
Brother	شقيق = أخ
To organize, arrange	رتّب، يرتّب
To pass by	مرّ، يمرّ على
Necessities	لوازم
Thus, in this Manner	هكذا
Responsibility	المسؤولية
To complain	شكا، يشكو
Struggle	الكفاح
Smile	بسمة
To pass	مضى، يمضي
Is still	مازال
Withstanding	صامدة
Courage	شجاعة
Patience	صبر

1- Answer the following questions:

– ماذا كانت ليلى تفعل قبل موت الأب والأم؟

_____

– ماذا تفعل ليلي الآن؟

_____

2- Try to find out the different expression of tenses one and classify them:

did	does	used to	was doing

3- Change the following structure according to the given pronouns:

كل يوم تستيقظ ليلى من نومها مبكرا.

أنا : _____

أنتم: _____

هو : _____

4- How did the writer begin each paragraph?

paragraph	connector	clarification

5- Write similar sentences following the given example:

‐ كانت ليلى ترتب البيت وتطبخ الطعام وتدرس شقيقها وشقيقتها , وهكذا كانت مسؤوليتها كبيرة.

‐ كان ـــــــــــــ و ـــــــــــــ و ـــــــــــ و وهكذا ـــــــــــــ

‐ كنت ـــــــــــــ و ـــــــــــــ و ـــــــــــ وهكذا ـــــــــــــ

‐ ـــ

‐ ـــ

6- The following phrases and sentences were cut from the text. Try to insert them in the right places.

– لتركب الباص

– يوما بعد يوم

– لتشتري لوازم الأسرة

– مبكرا

– كأي طفلة في عمرها

كانت تعيش مع والدها ووالدتها وأختها وأخيها وجدتها العجوز. كانت ليلى تقضي

وقتها في اللعب _____ . وفجأة مات الأب والأم في حادث, فوجدت ليلى

نفسها تواجه مشكله.

فجدتها العجوز تتحرك بصعوبة. وشقيقتها تبلغ الرابعة من عمرها . أما شقيقها

الصغير فيبلغ الثانية من عمره.

كل يوم تستيقظ ليلى من نومها _____ , فتعد طعام الإفطار لجدتها

العجوز وشقيقتها وشقيقها . وبعد ذلك ترتب البيت بسرعة ثم تسرع إلي الشارع

_____ وتذهب إلى المدرسة.

بعد أن تخرج من المدرسة تمر على السوق _____ , ثم تعود إلى البيت فتعد

الطعام وتذاكر دروسها.

وهكذا كانت المسؤولية كبيرة على الطفلة الصغيرة ..ولكنها لا تشكو بل تطيل ساعات

يومها وتقلل ساعات نومها لتخدم الأسرة.

وخلال هذا الكفاح اليومي لا تنسى ليلى أن تتحدث مع جدتها وتلعب مع شقيقها وتدرس

شقيقتها، وأكثر من ذلك، لا تنسى ليلى بسمتها مع الجميع .

وما زال الوقت يضيق ويمضي, ومازالت المسؤولية تزيد _____ , ومازالت

ليلى صامدة تتحمل المسؤولية بكل شجاعة وصبر .

7- Write sentences using the following connectors to express succession of actions:

الجملة	الأداة
	و
	ف
	ثم
	بعد
	بعد أن
	كما

Reflection:

Having completed this lesson, I know:

_____

_____

I still have trouble with the following:

_____

_____

I still need to know more about the following:

_____

_____

Homework الواجب:

There is a writing contest. Using some of the previous connectors, tenses, verbs, structures and phrases, write a story for the contest.

Self assessment:

Having completed this lesson, I am able to:

1- Narrate in the past.	( )
2- Narrate using different structures.	( )
3- Narrate using different tenses.	( )
4- Use connectors between sentences.	( )